"BAH, HUMBUG!"

First published in 1997 by Absolute Press
Scarborough House, 29 James Street West,
Bath, Somerset, England BA1 2BT
Tel: 01225 316013 Fax: 01225 445836

© Bah, Humbug, ABSOLUTE PRESS

Compiled by Andrew Langley
Cover Design by Christine Leech
Design by Katie Smith

Cover printed by Devenish & Co., Bath
Text printed by The Cromwell Press, Melksham

ISBN 1899791469

"BAH, HUMBUG!"

A Seasonal Antidote in Words and Pictures

Absolute Press

Christmas time!

That man must be a
misanthrope indeed,
in whose breast
something like a jovial
feeling is not aroused
in whose mind some
pleasant associations are
not awakened - by the
recurrence of Christmas.

Sketches By Boz
Charles Dickens

TO WISH
YOU · A
HAPPY
CHRISTMAS

"A Merry Christmas, uncle! God save you!" cried a cheerful voice. It was the voice of Scrooge's nephew, who came upon him so quickly that this was the first intimation he had of his approach.

"BAH!"

said Scrooge,

"HUMBUG!"

A Christmas Carol
Charles Dickens

"I'm afraid scratching that Monte Carlo trip has been a bit of a jar for you, Jeeves."

"Not at all, sir."

"Oh, yes, it has. The heart was set on wintering in the world's good old Plague Spot. I know. I saw your eye light up when I said we were due for a visit there. You snorted a bit and your fingers twitched. I know, I know. And now that there has been a change of programme the iron has entered into your soul."

"Not at all, sir."

"Oh, yes, it has. I've seen it. Very well then, what I wish to impress upon you, Jeeves, is that I have not been actuated in this matter by any mere idle whim. It was through no light and airy caprice that I accepted this invitation to Lady Wickham's. I have been angling for it for weeks, prompted by many considerations. In the first place, does one get the Yule-tide spirit at a spot like Monte Carlo?"

"Does one desire the Yule-tide spirit, sir?"

Jeeves And The Yule-Tide Spirit
P.G.Wodehouse

Everyone I suppose engaged in this irony of Xmas.

What a solemn lunatic the world is.

Journal Of A Disappointed Man
W.N.P.Barbellion

It seems to me that more should be known of the military postal science of causing Yuletide mortification, annoyance, irritation, inconvenience, vexation, offence, resentment and deep anger . . . The really big Christmas card can be immensely infuriating. It barges its way into your house, glows with the swank and pride of its sender, crowds everything off the mantlepiece and makes strangers cry "Ooooh" as they pick it up to see who is so rich, so powerful and so magnificent, as to be able to afford it. The very small Christmas card can be pretty insulting, too. Don't underestimate its destructive value. It shows what you think of the addressee - practically nothing.

Another intensely valuable and hurtful approach is the Out-Of-Season Touch. This studiously and carefully avoids robins, holly, snow, log-fires and wassail. People stuffed with Christmas pudding, South African port and crystallized ginger can be turned dizzy, green and reeling with the vertigoes by one glimpse of the front of a Christmas card of the Cutty-Sark in full sail. This number, which even in mid-summer is enough to give you the dry heaves, is available almost everywhere at a reasonable price. Strongly recommended and of great emetic value.

William Conner ('Cassandra' of The Daily Mirror)
21st December 1953

One Christmas I was at Longbridge and Christmas Day come and I was a bit homesick, you know, and had our Christmas Days dinner. I washed up and all that, and she said "Has tha finished now?" I said "Yes Madam" so she said, "Well if thou get all the paper there, you'll see a lot of paper there and there's a big needle there and a ball of string, if you go down to the paddock (that was the toilet) sit there and take the scissors and cut some paper up and thread it for the lavatory." And I sat there on Christmas Day and I think I cried a bucketful of tears. Christmas afternoon and I was sat . . . sitting cutting bits of paper like that . . . till about half past four when I went in for m'tea. Sitting there on the lavatory seat.

A Woman Servant in Lancashire in the 1900's
A Woman's Place
Elizabeth Roberts, 1984

Christmas

I went to bed at 1:30 and was kept awake till 4:30 by a barking dog. Then at 7:15 Mater knocked on the wall. She was in the middle of a bilious crisis caused by overnight hare and bilberries.

She stays in bed, hence the whole atmosphere of the house becomes special, and 'sick roomy', and I can't proceed with my novel today, as I had meant.

On Christmas Day of this year 1857 our villa saw a very unusual sight. My Father had given strictest charge that no difference whatever was to be made in our meals on that day; the dinner was to be neither more copious than usual nor less so. He was obeyed, but the servants, secretly rebellious, made a small plum-pudding for themselves. Early in the afternoon, the maids - of whom we were now advanced to keeping two - kindly remarked that 'the poor dear child ought to have a bit, anyhow,' and wheedled me into the kitchen, where I ate a slice of plum-pudding.

Shortly I began to feel that pain inside which in my frail state was inevitable, and my conscience smote me violently. At length I could bear my spiritual anguish no longer, and bursting into the study I called out: "Oh! Papa, Papa, I have eaten of flesh offered to idols!" It took some time, between my sobs, to explain what had happened. Then my father sternly said: "Where is the accursed thing?" I explained that as much as was left of it was still on the kitchen table. He took me by the hand, and ran with me into the midst of the startled servants, seized what remained of the pudding, and with the plate in one hand and me still tight in the other, ran till we reached the dust-heap, when he flung the idolatrous confectionery onto the middle of the ashes, and then raked it deep into the mass. The suddenness, the violence, the velocity of this extraordinary act made an impression on my memory which nothing will ever efface.

Father And Son
Edmund Gosse

1927

I'm sick of Jesus, and don't see at all why he

should go on being born every year.

The Letters of D.H.Lawrence

"You have heard of fossilized substances?" Simpson began, in that rasping voice so familiar to his pupils at the S.V.P.

I nodded across my briar.

"Well," he continued, "it has always been a pet theory of mine that, just as a substance can, by the action of certain alkaloids operating in the course of time, become, to all purposes, metallic, so - you follow me - it can, in like manner, be restored to its previous condition. You have heard of plum-puddings being kept for twenty-one years?"

I nodded; less, I am afraid, in assent than owing to a physical cause.

"Well," I heard him saying, "the stuff that you have eaten tonight is about two hundred and fifty years old and may be much more than that, at a very moderate computation."

I started. Simpson had raised his voice rather suddenly. He took my start for surprise and continued wagging his crippled forefinger at me. "That pudding was originally a cannon-ball. It was picked up on the field of Naseby. Never mind how I came by it. It has been under treatment in my laboratory for the last ten years."

The Defossilized Christmas Pudding
Max Beerbohm, The Saturday Review, 1896

Idolatrie in crust! Babylon's whore
Rak'd from the grave, and bak'd by hanches, then
Sew'd up in Coffins to unholy men;
Defil'd, with superstition, like the Gentiles
Of old, that worshipp'd onions, roots, and lentiles!

Christmas Day
Giles Fletcher, 1656

Sunday, Christmas Day

It was an intense frost. I sat down in my bath upon a sheet of thick ice which broke in the middle into large pieces whilst sharp points and jagged edges stuck all round the sides of the tub like chevaux de frise, not particularly comforting to the naked thighs and loins, for the keen ice cut like broken glass. The ice water stung and scorched like fire. I had to collect the floating pieces of ice and pile them on a chair before I could use the sponge and then I had to thaw the sponge in my hands for it was a mass of ice.

The Diary of The Rev. Francis Kilvert
Edited by William Plomer

A Christmas family party!

We know nothing in
nature more delightful!

Sketches By Boz
Charles Dickens

What an afternoon! **Mr Gummidge said that, in his estimation, there never had been such an afternoon since the world began, a sentiment which was heartily endorsed by Mrs Gummidge and all the little Gummidges, not to mention the relatives who had come over from Jersey for the day.

In the first place, there was the ennui. And such ennui it was! A heavy, overpowering ennui, such as results from a participation in eight courses of steaming, gravied food, topping off with salted nuts which the little old spinster Gummidge from Oak Hill said she never knew when to stop eating - and true enough she didn't - a dragging, devitalising ennui, which left its victims strewn about the living room in various states of prostration suggestive of those of the petrified occupants in a newly unearthed Pompeian dwelling; an ennui which carried with it a retinue of yawns, snarls and thinly veiled insults, and which ended in ruptures in the clan spirit serious enough to last throughout the glad new year.

And the cigar smoke! Mrs Gummidge said that she didn't mind the smoke from a good cigarette, but would they mind if she opened the windows for just a minute in order to clear the room of the heavy aroma of used cigars? Mr Gummidge stoutly maintained that they were good cigars. His brother, George Gummidge, said that he, likewise, would say that they were.

Christmas Afternoon; Done in the Manner, if not the Spirit, of Dickens.
Robert Benchley

1893

It really is an atrocious institution, this Christmas. We must be gluttonous because it is Christmas. We must be drunken because it is Christmas. We must be insincerely generous; we must buy things that nobody wants, and give them to people we don't like; we must go to absurd entertainments that make even our little children satirical; we must writhe under venal officiousness from legions of freebooters, all because it is Christmas.

The World, 20 December 1893
George Bernard Shaw

The annual invitation came to spend Christmas with Carrie's mother - the usual family festive gathering to which we always look forward. Lupin declined to go. I was astounded, and expressed my surprise and disgust. Lupin then obliged us with the following Radical speech:

"I hate a family gathering at Christmas. What does it mean? Why, someone says: 'Ah! We miss poor Uncle James, who was here last year,' and we all begin to snivel. Someone else says: 'It's two years since poor Aunt Liz used to sit in that corner.' Then we all begin to snivel again. Then another gloomy relation says: 'Ah! I wonder whose turn it will be next?' Then we all snivel again, and proceed to eat and drink too much; and they don't discover until I get up that we have been seated thirteen at dinner."

The Diary Of A Nobody
George and Weedon Grossmith

[The terrifying GREEN KNIGHT gatecrashes King Arthur's Christmas Dinner at Camelot. In response to a challenge, Sir Gawain cuts off the visitor's head. The Green Knight calmly picks up the appendage . . .]

For the head in his hand he holds up straight,
Toward the noblest lady on the dais he turns the face,
And it lifts up its eyelids in a broad stare,
And speaks thus with its mouth, as you may now hear:

"Look, Gawain, you be ready as you promised,
And look for me faithfully, sir, until you find me,
As you have sworn in this hall, before these knights.
To the Green Chapel you shall go, I charge you, to receive
Just such a blow as you have dealt,
To be promptly given on New Year's morn.
Many men know the Knight of the Green Chapel,
So if you ask you cannot fail to find me.
Therefore come, or you must be called a coward!"
With a violent jerk he turns the reins,
Gallops out of the hall, his head in his hand,
And the sparks fly from the stones under his horse's hooves.

Sir Gawain and the Green Knight
Middle English Poem

The Vindication Of Christmas:
An Anonymous Seventeenth Century Broadsheet

Christmas Day! I hate the vulgar revelry which usually accompanies it - the fat beef, the gross turkeys, the stuffed sausage, as evidences of human joy at the Salvation of Christ - are to me utterly disgusting! - But my boys will consider me a brute if I don't eat till I can't see, to prove my joy at their presence.

The Diaries of Benjamin Robert Haydon

"Fire!" cried Mrs Prothero,

and she beat the dinner-gong. And we ran down the garden, with the snowballs in our arms, toward the house; and smoke, indeed, was pouring out of the dining-room, and the gong was bombilating, and Mrs Prothero was announcing ruin like a town crier in Pompeii.

Something was burning alright; perhaps it was Mr Prothero, who always slept there after midday dinner with the newspaper over his face. But he was standing in the middle of the room, saying, "A fine Christmas!" and smacking at the smoke with a slipper. "Call the fire brigade," cried Mrs Prothero as she beat the gong.

"They won't be there," said Mr Prothero, "It's Christmas."

There was no fire to be seen, only clouds of smoke and Mr Prothero standing in the middle of them, waving his slipper as though he were conducting.

"Do something," he said.

And we threw all our snowballs into the smoke - I think we missed Mr Prothero - and ran out of the house to the telephone box.

"Let's call the police as well," Jim said.

"And the ambulance."

"And Ernie Jenkins, he likes fires."

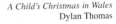

A Child's Christmas in Wales
Dylan Thomas

1661 Christmas Day

Dined at home all alone. And taking occasion, from some fault in the meat, to complain of my maid's Sluttery, my wife and I fell out, and I up to my Chamber in a discontent . . .

1662

Up pretty early, leaving my wife not well in bed . . .

1663

Lay long, talking pleasantly with my wife; but among other things, she begin, I know not whether by design or chance, to enquire what she should do if I should by an accident die . . .

1664

Up (my wife's eye being ill still of the blow I did in a passion give her on Monday last) to church alone . . .

1665

To church in the morning, and there saw a wedding in the church, which I have not seen many a day, and the young people so merry one with another; and strange, to see what delight we married people have to see these poor fools decoyed into our condition . . .

The Diary of Samuel Pepys
Edited by Robert Latham

t is Christmas Day in the Workhouse,
And the cold bare walls are bright
With garlands of green and holly,
And the place is a pleasant sight:
For with clean-washed hands and faces,
In a long and hungry line
The paupers sit at the tables,
For this is the hour they dine.

 nd the guardians and their ladies,
Although the wind is east,
Have come in their furs and wrappers,
To watch their charges feast;
To smile and be condescending,
Put pudding on pauper plates,
To be hosts at the workhouse banquet
They've paid for - with the rates.

Christmas Day in the Workhouse
George R. Sims

Meshed, Persia

Xmas Day reproduced itself even here - a dull
drizzly day, too much for lunch, that sick feeling at
tea, and a nightmare of a party in the evening
followed by highly organised parlour games for all.
I had the unforeseeable misfortune to win 1st prize.
It was appalling. Even now I would have preferred
to spend the day by myself in a caravanserai.

The letters of Robert Byron

[The narrator, Good Time Charley and Dancing Dan make their way up Broadway after drinking large amounts of hot Tom and Jerry. Dan is dressed as Father Christmas.]

As we go up Broadway, headed for Forty-ninth Street, Charley and I see many citizens we know and give them a large hello, and wish them Merry Christmas, and some of these citizens shake hands with Santa Claus, not knowing he is nobody but Dancing Dan, although later I understand there is some gossip among these citizens because they claim a Santa Claus with such a breath on him as our Santa Claus has is a little out of line.

And once we are somewhat embarrassed when a lot of little kids going home with their parents from a late Christmas party somewhere gather about Santa Claus with shouts of childish glee, and some of them wish to climb up Santa Claus's legs. Naturally, Santa Claus gets a little peevish, and calls them a few names, and one of the parents comes up and wishes to know what is the idea of Santa Claus using such language, and

Santa Claus takes a punch at the parent, all of
which is no doubt most astonishing to the little
kids who have an idea of Santa Claus as a very
kindly old guy. But of course they do not know
about Dancing Dan mixing the liquor we get in
the spots we visit with his Tom and Jerry, or they
will understand how even Santa Claus can lose
his temper.

Dancing Dan's Christmas
Damon Runyon

my christmas
Mum's Christmas

decoration
climbing up to the loft on a wobbly ladder,
probably falling.

a christmas tree
pine needles and tinsel all over the carpet.

lots of food
preparations and loads of dishes to be washed.

crackers
crumpled paper everywhere.

presents
money down the drain.

sweets
indigestion and toothache.

parties
late nights, and driving back through the dark.

snow to play in
getting soaked and frozen whenever outside.

A poem by Sarah Hodgson
A Child's View of Christmas

1945

Christmas

By keeping the children in bed
for long periods we managed to
have a tolerable day.

1946

Christmas

I made a fair show of geniality
throughout the day though the
spectacle of a litter of shoddy
toys and half eaten sweets
sickened me . . . a ghastly day.

The Diaries of Evelyn Waugh

There seems a magic in the very name of Christmas. Petty jealousies and discords are forgotten; social feelings are awakened, in bosoms to which they have long been strangers.

Sketches By Boz
Charles Dickens

"**If** I could work my will," said Scrooge indignantly, "every idiot who goes about with 'Merry Christmas' on his lips, should be boiled with his own pudding, and buried with a stake of holly through his heart."

A Christmas Carol
Charles Dickens

A homely pleasure - to receive
A hamper upon Christmas Eve;
To know that someone kindly thinks
Of Norwood, and Professor Jinks.

Who sent it? - not my brother Jim -
I'm not on speaking terms with him.
My sister Caroline - ah,no!
I quarrelled with her long ago.

It might have been my cousin Kate,
Only we've not been friends of late;
Aunt Harrison or Uncle Clem,
But then I've had a row with them.

Let's cut the string! No card or name -
Will it be turkey, goose or game? . . .
An unfledged chick - of straggling limb!
It must be from that scoundrel Jim.

Anonymous Victorian Poem
A Celebration Of Christmas
Gillian Cooke

1983

I have long thought it a pity that Scrooge, like so many people in Dickens, spoilt his case by overstatement. To dismiss the Christmas spirit as humbug will not quite do as it stands, but it gets close. All those presents, ingenious devices for taking money off you for things other people don't want in return for things you don't want yourself, in fact you often don't just not want them, you find them positively offensive. So that's the kind of book/tie/bottle of booze/gadget they think I'd appreciate, you mutter aggrievedly.

Then there's the points-for-trouble-taken system used by wives on your present to them, whereby a diamond necklace scores zero if ordered by telephone and paid for through the post, with something like a maximum score for a Cannibal Island nose-ring obtained on the spot in person.

Christmas
Kingsley Amis

Poirot pursued his theme: "And families now, families who have been separated throughout the year, assemble once more together. Now under these conditions, my friend, you must admit that there will occur a great deal of strain. People who do not feel amiable are putting great pressure on themselves to appear amiable! There is at Christmas-time a great deal of hypocrisy, hypocrisy undertaken 'pour le bon motif', c'est entendu, but nevertheless hypocrisy."

"Well, I shouldn't put it quite like that myself," said Colonel Johnson doubtfully.

Poirot beamed upon him.

"No, no. It is I who am putting it like that, not you. I am pointing out to you that under these conditions it is highly probable that dislikes that were before merely mild and disagreements that were trivial might suddenly assume a more serious character. The result of pretending to be a more amiable, a more forgiving, a more high-minded person than one really is has sooner or later the effect of causing one to behave as a more disagreeable, a more ruthless and an altogether more unpleasant person than is actually the case! If you dam the stream of natural behaviour, mon ami, sooner or later the dam bursts and a cataclysm occurs!"

Hercule Poirot's Christmas
Agatha Christie

I am a poor man, but I would gladly give ten shillings to find out who sent me the insulting Christmas card I received this morning. I never insult people; why should they insult me? The worst part of the transaction is, that I find myself suspecting all my friends. The handwriting on the envelope is evidently disguised, being written sloping the wrong way. I cannot think either Gowing or Cummings would do such a mean thing. Lupin denied all knowledge of it; although I disapprove of his laughing and sympathizing with the offender. Mr Franching would be above such an act; and I don't think any of the Mutlars would descend to such a course. I wonder if Pitt, that impudent clerk at the office, did it? Or Mrs Birrell, the charwoman, or Burwin-Fosselton? The writing is too good for the former.

The Diary of a Nobody
George And Weedon Grossmith

King John was not a good man,
And no good friends had he.
He stayed in every afternoon . . .
But no one came to tea.
And, round about December,
The cards upon his shelf
Which wished lots of Christmas cheer,
And fortune in the coming year,
Were never from his near and dear,
But only from himself.

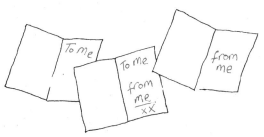

King John's Christmas
A.A.Milne

1911

On the way to the South Pole

Scott got fairly wound up and went on and on . . .
My breath kept fogging my glasses, and our
windproofs got oppressively warm and altogether
things were pretty rotten. At last he stopped and we
found we had done fourteen and three-quarter miles.

He said, "What about fifteen miles for Christmas
Day?", so we gladly went on - anything definite is
better than indefinite trudging.

The Diary of Henry "Birdy" Bowers

We would have Spent this day of the nativity of
Christ in feasting, had we anything either to raise
our Sperits or even gratify our appetites, our Diner
consisting of pore Elk, so much Spoiled that we eate
it thro' mear necessity, Some Spoiled pounded fish
and a few roots.

Journal of William Clark,
Second-in-Command of the Lewis and Clark Expedition to the USA's Pacific Coast

[William has sworn to be truthful throughout Christmas. He finds it difficult, especially when a grand visitor calls.]

Lady Atkinson was stout and elderly and wore a very youthful hat and coat.

"I've brought you my Christmas present in person," she said in the tone of voice of one giving an unheard-of treat. "Look!"

She took out of an envelope a large signed photograph of herself. "There now . . . what do you think of that?"

Murmurs of surprise and admiration and gratitude. Lady Atkinson drank them in complacently.

"It's very good, isn't it? You . . . little boy . . . don't you think it's very like me?"

William gazed at it critically.

"It's not as fat as you are," was his final offering on the altar of truth.

"William!" screamed Mrs Brown,
"How can you be so impolite!"

"Impolite?" said William with some indignation.
"I'm not tryin' to be polite! I'm bein' truthful.
It isn't 's fat as what she is," he went on doggedly,
"An' it's not got as many little lines on its face as
what she has an' its different lookin' altogether.
It looks pretty an' she doesn't - "

Lady Atkinson towered over him,
quivering with rage.

"You nasty little boy!" she said, thrusting her face
close to his. "You - NASTY - little - boy!"

William's Truthful Christmas
Richmal Crompton

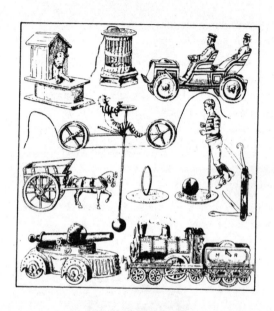

Christmas Gift Suggestions
Chatterbox, 1908

· CHRISTMAS SHOPPING ·

Spending beyond their income on gifts for Christmas -

Swing door and crowded lifts and drapery jungles -

What shall we buy for our husbands and sons

       Different from last year?

Foxes hang by their noses behind the plate glass -

Screams of macaws across festoons of paper -

Only the faces on the boxes of chocolates are free

       From boredom and crows feet.

Christmas Shopping
Louis MacNeice

A CHRISTMAS TRAGEDY

A London lady, on Boxing Night, was entertaining some friends, and appeared herself in the costume of Winter. She was dressed in a white robe of thin fabric, and stood under a canopy from which fell pieces of cotton wool to represent snowflakes, and in their descent one of them caught light at the candelabra, and fell at the deceased's feet. In trying to put it out with her foot her dress caught fire, and she was immediately enveloped in flames. So inflammable was the material that, although prompt assistance was rendered, she was so severely burned as to become unconscious. A medical man was sent for, and everything possible was done for her; but she sank gradually, and died from exhaustion.

Christmas, its Origins and Associations
Rev.W.F.Dawson

While I watch the Christmas blaze
Paint the room with ruddy rays,
Something makes my vision glide
To the frosty scene outside.

There, to reach a rotting berry,
Toils a thrush - constrained to very
Dregs of food by sharp distress,
Taking such with thankfulness.

Why, O starving bird, when I
One day's joy would justify,
And put misery out of view,
Do you make me notice you?

The Reminder
Thomas Hardy

I have something which makes it all bearable, the presents, the in-laws, other peoples' children, your own children, the games, the noise, the mess, the ridiculous meals. It consists of one part French cooking brandy, one part Irish whiskey and four parts fresh milk. The hard part is remembering to have put milk instead of water into one of your ice trays the previous night. Drink the mixture immediately on rising, while the others are having breakfast or throwing up behind the snowman.

Christmas
Kingsley Amis

Would that Christmas lasted
the whole year through!

Sketches By Boz
Charles Dickens

Acknowledgements

The publishers would like to acknowledge the following illustration sources:

'Small Ones, Stock Blocks'   Garret & Atkinson
Curious Woodcuts of Fanciful and Real Beasts   Konrad Gesner (Dover, 1971)
Illustrations pages 20 & 60   Patrick H. Insole
Christmas Gift Suggestions   Chatterbox, 1908